NATIONAL GEOGRAPHIC

Go West!

Reyna Eisenstark

PICTURE CREDITS

Cover © Phil Schermeister/CORBIS; title page, page 4 © New York Public Library/Art Resource, NY; pages 2-3, 34-d © Lester Lefkowitz/CORBIS; pages 4-5, 8, 14 (top), 30 (top right) illustrations by Rose Zgodzinski; pages 5, 18 (bottom), 22-23 (bottom), 25 (top left), 26 (bottom), 34-c © The Granger Collection; pages 6-7 © Coffrin's Old West Gallery; pages 9, 36 © Smithsonian Institution Press; page 9 (top) © Courtesy of Mrs. John F. Clymer and the Clymer Museum of Art; pages 10 (top), 11 © Smithsonian American Art Museum, Washington, DC/ Art Resource, NY; page 10 (bottom) © Gunter Marx Photography/CORBIS; page 12 (top) © Minnesota Historical Society/CORBIS; page 12 (inset) © Neal Mishler/Getty Images; pages 12-13, 35-b © The Bridgeman Art Library; pages 14 (bottom), 32 © Michael T. Sedam/CORBIS; page 15 © Layne Kennedy/CORBIS; pages 16-17, 30 (bottom left), 35-c © Jan Butchofsky-Houser/CORBIS; pages 18-19 (top), 25 (top right), 31 (bottom left) © Annie Griffiths Belt/CORBIS; pages 19 (bottom right), 20-21 (bottom), 25 (bottom left), 31 (top left), 34-b Courtesy The Library of Congress; page 20-21 (top) © CORBIS; page 21 (bottom right) © Michael S. Quinton/National Geographic/Getty Images; pages 22-23 (top) © Oregon Historical Society; page 25 (bottom right) © Hulton Deutsch Collection/CORBIS; page 26 (top) © Jim and Mary Whitmer; pages 27 (top), 27 (bottom), 29 (top), 30 (bottom right) © Bettmann/CORBIS; page 28 (top left) © Dan Bartruff/CORBIS; page 28 (top right) © Scott T. Smith/CORBIS; page 28 (bottom left) © Owaki-Kulla/CORBIS; page 28 (bottom right) © Premium Stock/CORBIS; page 29 (bottom) © David Young-Wolff/PhotoEdit; pages 30 (top left), 31 (bottom right) © David Muench/CORBIS; page 31 (top right) © Steve and Mary Skjold/Index Stock Imagery; pages 31 (center left), 35-a Courtesy of The Bureau of Land Management, Wyoming; page 31 (center right) © Chris Carroll/CORBIS; page 33 (left) *Our Journey West* by Gare Thompson, © 2002 National Geographic Society, photos © Scotts Bluff National Monument, (center) *The West* by Gare Thompson, © 2003 National Geographic Society, photos © Hulton Archive/Getty Images, (right) *Building the Transcontinental Railroad* by Monica Halpern, © 2002 National Geographic Society, photos (inset) © Abbey Aldrich Rockefeller Folk Art Center, Williamsburg VA, (background) © Union Pacific Historical Collection; page 34-a © The Barnes Foundation/The Bridgeman Art Library; page 35-d © The Detroit Institute of Arts/The Bridgeman Art Library.

Produced through the worldwide resources of the National Geographic Society, John M. Fahey, Jr., President and Chief Executive Officer; Gilbert M. Grosvenor, Chairman of the Board; Nina D. Hoffman, Executive Vice President and President, Books and Education Publishing Group.

PREPARED BY NATIONAL GEOGRAPHIC SCHOOL PUBLISHING

Ericka Markman, Senior Vice President and President, Children's Books and Education Publishing Group; Steve Mico, Senior Vice President, Editorial Director, Publisher; Francis Downey, Executive Editor; Richard Easby, Editorial Manager; Anne Stone, Lori Dibble Collins, Editors; Bea Jackson, Director of Layout and Design; Jim Hiscott, Design Manager; Cynthia Olson, Art Director; Margaret Sidlosky, Illustrations Director; Matt Wascavage, Manager of Publishing Services; Sean Philpotts, Jane Ponton, Production Managers; Ted Tucker, Production Specialist.

MANUFACTURING AND QUALITY CONTROL

Christopher A. Liedel, Chief Financial Officer; Phillip L. Schlosser, Director; Clifton M. Brown III, Manager

◀ The Rocky Mountains stood in the way of people moving west.

Contents

CONSULTANT AND REVIEWER
Dr. Peter Hinks, Historian, Wethersfield, Connecticut

BOOK DESIGN/PHOTO RESEARCH
Steve Curtis Design, Inc.

Published by the National Geographic Society
1145 17th Street N.W.
Washington, D.C. 20036-4688

ISBN-10: 0-7922-5446-5
ISBN-13: 978-0-7922-5446-1

2022 2021 2020 2019 2018
3 4 5 6 7 8 9 10 11 12 13 14 15

Printed in the United States of America

A Growing Nation

In the early 1800s, the United States was different than today. For example, there were fewer states. At the time, all of the states were between the Atlantic Ocean and the Mississippi River.

Many people wanted to move west of the Mississippi River. They wanted to make better lives for themselves. People called the land west of the Mississippi River the West.

◀ **Some families moved to the West where there were fewer people.**

Many people lived in cities in the United States in the early 1800s.

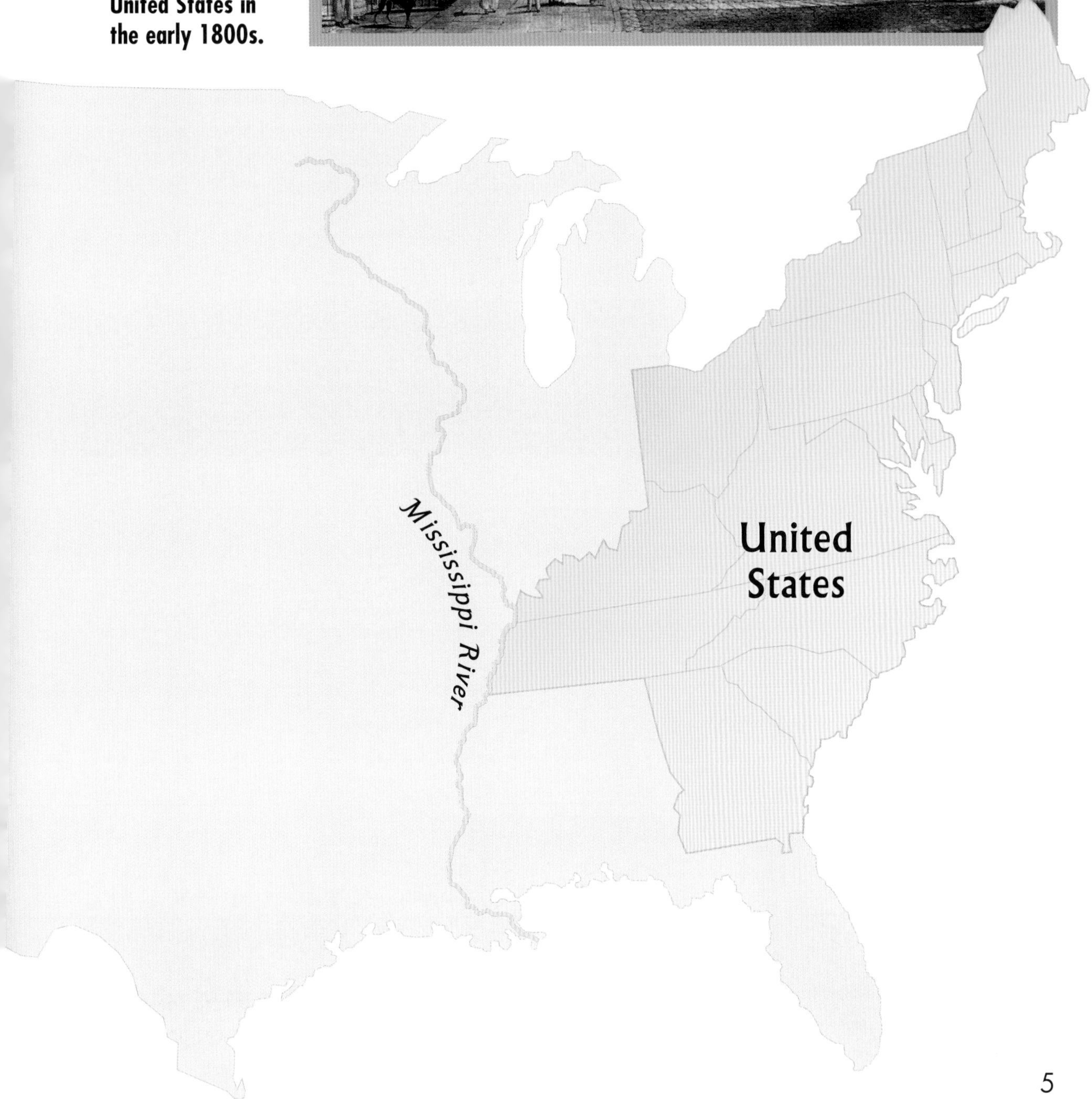

1 Understand the Big Idea

The Move

Big Idea

In the 1800s, many Americans moved to the West to make better lives.

Set Purpose

Learn how and why many Americans moved west in the 1800s.

Questions You Will Explore

Why did people move to the American West in the 1800s?

How did they get there?

West

In the early 1800s, the United States was still a young nation. All the states were east of the Mississippi River.

The land in the West was a **frontier**. Native Americans already lived there. Yet the promise of land and riches soon brought many more people.

By the 1840s, thousands of people made the trip each year. They traveled by horse, by wagon, and on foot.

frontier – unexplored land at the edge of a settled area

▲ Wagons carried supplies to people who moved west.

▲ The map shows the Louisiana Purchase.

A Growing Nation

President Thomas Jefferson bought land from France in 1803. The land was in North America. It was a large area west of the Mississippi River. People named Jefferson's land deal the Louisiana Purchase.

▲ **Lewis and Clark's journey was not easy. There were dangers, such as bears.**

Lewis and Clark

All the land west of the Mississippi River was called the West. Most Americans, however, did not know much about the area. Some books told amazing tales. Some even told of unicorns living there!

To learn the truth, President Jefferson sent a team to explore the West. Meriwether Lewis and William Clark led the **expedition**.

▲ **Lewis and Clark used this compass.**

expedition – a journey or trip to explore a new place

▲ **Native Americans hunted buffalo in the West.**

Who Lived in the West?

Lewis and Clark met Native Americans on their journey. Many Native American groups, or **tribes**, lived in the West. They included the Shoshone and Nez Perce tribes.

Some of the tribes lived in tents. Others lived in grass huts. They hunted fish, birds, buffalo, and other animals.

▲ **Many Native Americans made their homes from the skins of animals they hunted.**

tribe – a group of people or families living together

▲ **People traveling west met Native Americans.**

Native Americans

People traveling west often met Native Americans. The tribes were often friendly. They would help **settlers** if their wagons got stuck or if their cattle wandered away.

However, these meetings were not always friendly. As more settlers moved west, some tribes grew fearful of losing their land and way of life. Native Americans and settlers sometimes fought bloody battles over land.

settler – a person who moves to an undeveloped area to live

▼ A gold miner

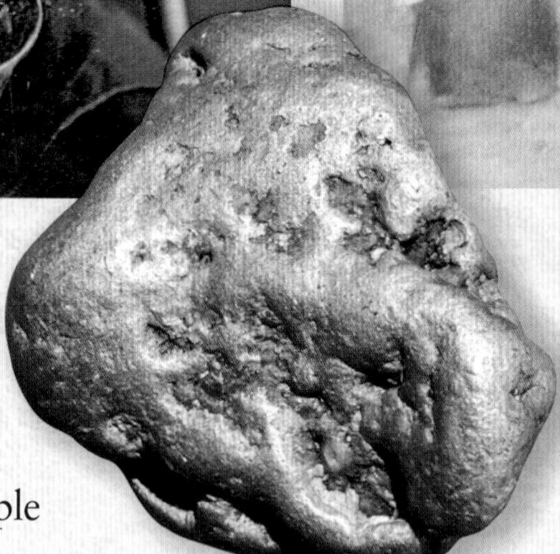
▲ A gold nugget

The Gold Rush

Most early settlers moved west for farmland. Then in the late 1840s, a new discovery **drew** people west. In 1848, people discovered gold in California. The next year thousands of people rushed there to dig for gold. They were called "forty-niners." Can you guess why?

Towns quickly sprang up across California. Some grew into cities. California became a state in 1850.

draw – to attract

▲ These settlers are in front of their home. It was built into the side of a hill.

Land for Free

By the 1860s, much of the gold was gone. But people kept moving west. Now they came for land. The West had lots of land!

In 1862, the United States government passed the **Homestead Act**. This law gave land to anyone older than 21. All a person had to do was live on the land and farm it for five years.

Many people began to make the trip west. How would they get there?

Homestead Act – a law that gave land to settlers

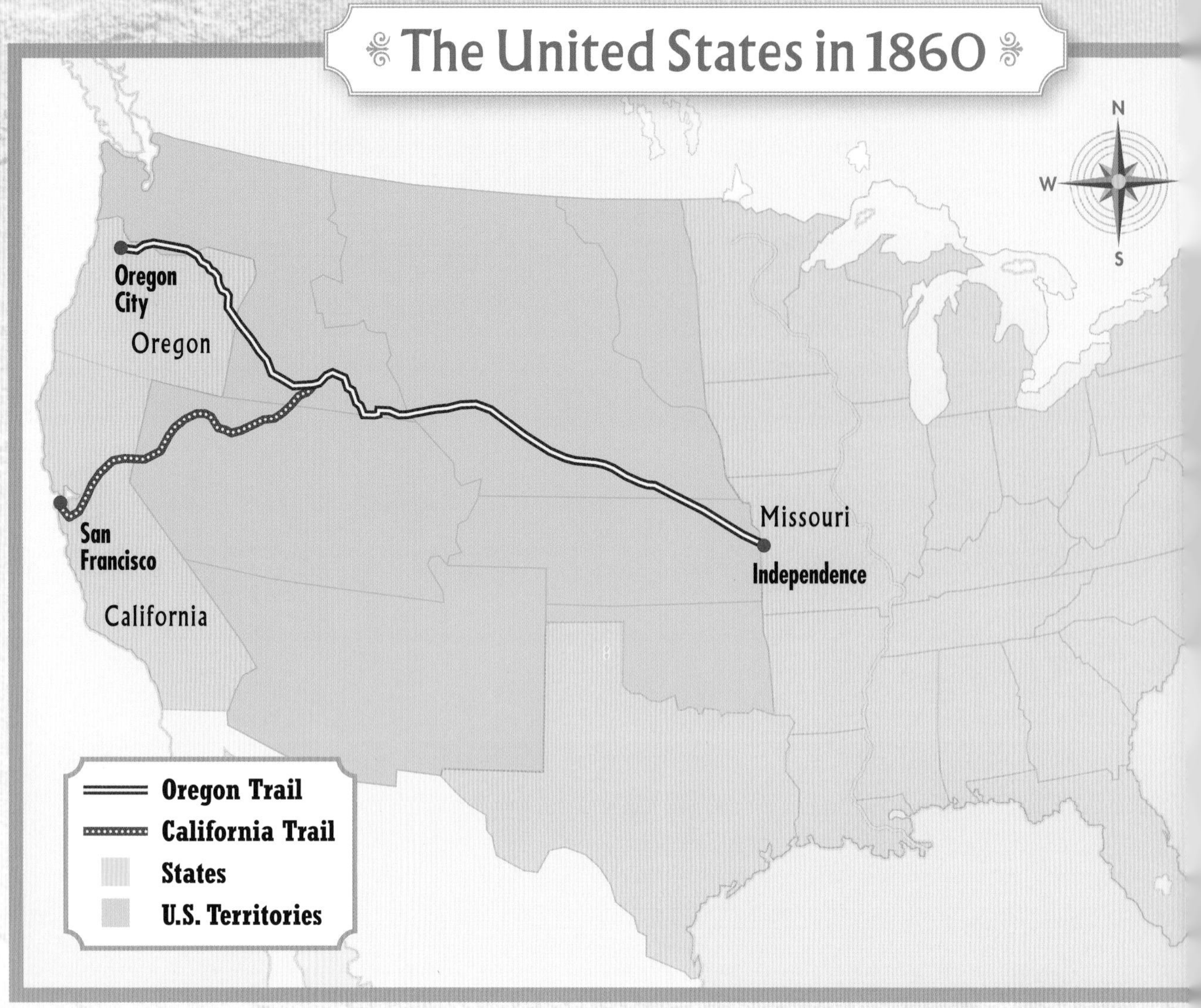

▲ The map shows the trails settlers followed to the West.

Riding the Oregon Trail

Settlers followed two main trails to the West. Many took the Oregon Trail. It was 2,000 miles long. It went from Independence, Missouri, to Oregon.

Other settlers took the California Trail. It split from the Oregon Trail. It led to towns and gold mines in California.

Many settlers on both trails rode in covered wagons. Some settlers brought everything they owned in the wagons.

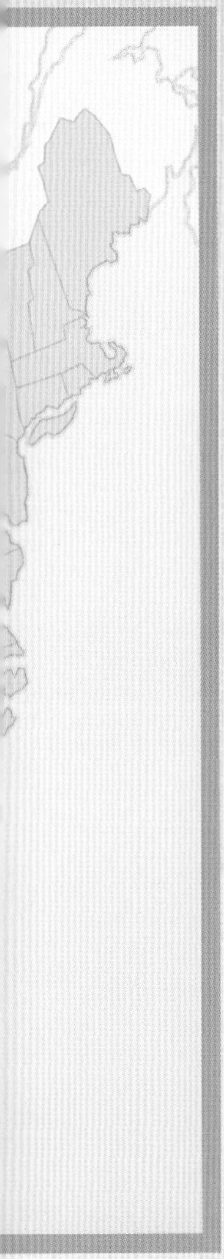

▲ Settlers moved west in covered wagons.

A Difficult Journey

Settlers faced many **hardships** on the trail. The trip could take four months or longer. Many people died along the way.

Still many families took the chance. They risked their lives for free land, gold, and the promise of better lives. These people built houses, farms, and towns. Before long, new states formed in the West.

Stop and Think!

Why did settlers move to the West in the 1800s?

hardship – a problem

2 Take a **Closer Look**

Recap
Explain why settlers moved to the West.

Set Purpose
Now read about one family's journey to the West.

SARAH

In 1852, Sarah Sprenger's family left their home in Ohio to move west. Sarah was ten years old at the time. The family traveled by covered wagon. The trip took six months. Sarah wrote about the journey many years later. Here are some of her memories.

This story is adapted from the memories of Sarah Sprenger.

'S JOURNEY

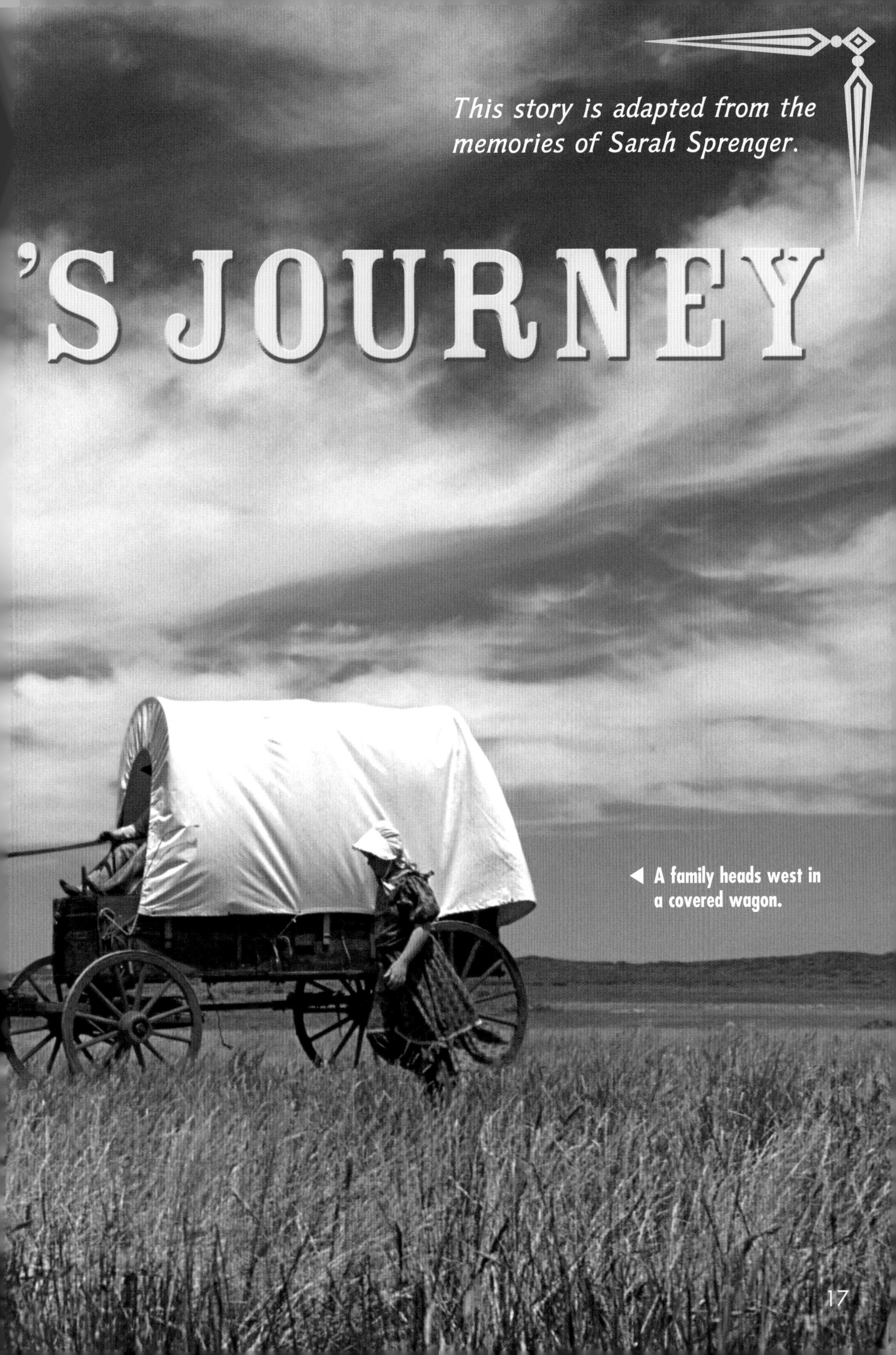

◀ **A family heads west in a covered wagon.**

LEAVING HOME

My brother Abraham moved to Oregon in 1850. He wrote letters to Mother and Father. The letters told about Oregon. My parents liked what they read. They decided we would move there the following spring.

We spent all winter getting ready. Father and Mother loaded our things into three wagons. One was made for us to ride in. It had a door and steps at the back. Finally, on April 1, 1852, we set out for Oregon.

▲ This painting shows St. Joseph, Missouri, in the mid-1800s.

GATHERING SUPPLIES

We did not go straight to Oregon. We stopped in St. Joseph, Missouri, for supplies. We stayed there for six weeks.

Father spent the time gathering supplies for the rest of the trip. He bought bedding, tents, and food. He also bought a cow for milk. Father bought four oxen to pull our wagon. The oxen are much stronger than horses. We were on our way again by the middle of May.

▲ People carried everything they needed in a covered wagon.

▲ People shopped in general stores like this one.

ON THE TRAIL

Every day I saw something new on the trail. We saw buffalo and antelope. Once in a while we would kill one. Antelope meat is delicious!

When our cow gave extra milk, we put the milk in a big tin can. We hung the can on the wagon. The bumping along the trail **churned** the milk into butter.

churn – to mix or stir milk to make butter

▼ **Native Americans stand in front of their tepees.**

HARD TIMES

We often saw Native Americans. Once a Nez Perce chief offered Father some horses. The chief wanted to trade the horses for my sister Maria! Father said no.

Later my sister Abbie became sick. A doctor from a nearby town sat up with Father and Mother caring for Abbie. He could not help her. She died.

▼ **Buffalo cross a river in Wyoming.**

◀ **Antelope**

RIVER CROSSING

When we got close to Oregon, we had to cross the Green River. We unloaded two of the wagons. We tied our beds together with rope. Then a few boys swam across the river. They tied a rope to a tree. We loaded the beds with food. Father and the boys pulled the beds across the river.

▼ **This photograph shows Oregon City in the 1850s.**

▼ **Settlers pull their wagon across a river.**

OREGON CITY

We finally arrived in Oregon City on October 26, 1852. The whole journey took six months. It was a hard trip. But we were glad we made it. We would have a new life in the West. I looked forward to seeing my brother Abraham.

Stop and Think!

What was the journey to the West like?

3 Make Connections

Recap

Tell how and why people moved west in the 1800s.

Set Purpose

Read to learn more about the West.

CONNECT WHAT YOU HAVE LEARNED

Go West!

In the early 1800s, all of the states were east of the Mississippi River. Some people moved west in search of gold. Others moved west for land. So many people moved west that new states formed in the area.

Here are some ideas that you learned about the West.

- President Jefferson bought the Louisiana Territory in 1803.
- Settlers moved to the West.
- Settlers found gold in California in 1848.
- New states formed in the West.

Check What You Have Learned

Why did people move to the American West in the 1800s?

▲ Lewis and Clark led an expedition to explore the West.

▲ Families moved west in covered wagons.

▲ Many people moved to the West to look for gold.

▲ So many people moved west that new states formed in the area.

Birth of Blue Jeans

Did you know that blue jeans were invented in California? In 1853, Levi Strauss heard about the California gold rush. He moved to the West, but not to pan for gold. He started a business selling goods to gold miners.

In the 1870s, Jacob Davis brought Strauss an idea for sturdy pants. Davis and Strauss became partners, and people all over bought these new pants. They are what we call "blue jeans" today.

▼ **Levi Strauss employees in San Francisco**

▲ Rider on the Pony Express

The Pony Express

After moving to the West, settlers tried to stay in contact with people they left behind. How could they send mail? Many used the Pony Express. The Pony Express started in 1860. Horses and riders carried mail back and forth across the West.

▲ A letter sent by the Pony Express

The trail was about 2,000 miles. Riders carried a bag of mail for 75 to 100 miles. Then they would stop and give the mail to the next rider. Later, trains and other technology replaced the Pony Express.

CONNECT TO TRANSPORTATION

Faster and Faster

How would you and your family travel across the country? Would you take a covered wagon? Probably not!

Use this chart to compare travel today with travel in the 1800s. Which is the fastest? How would you like to make the trip?

TIME TO CROSS THE UNITED STATES

covered wagon 1800s

about 6 months

railroad 1870s

about 10 days

car today

about 7 days

passenger jet today

about 5 hours

▶ Laura Ingalls Wilder

Frontier Girl

For years, books written by Laura Ingalls Wilder have told what life was like in the West. Her "Little House" books tell the true story of a young girl and her family in the late 1800s.

Wilder was born in 1867 in a log cabin in Wisconsin. Then her family traveled west by covered wagon. They lived in Kansas, Minnesota, and South Dakota.

As an adult, Wilder often told her grandchildren about her childhood. They asked her to write the stories so other children could enjoy them.

Zoom in on Words

Many kinds of words are used in this book. Here you will learn about proper nouns. You will also learn about words that have more than one meaning.

Proper Nouns

A proper noun is a word that names a specific person, place, or thing. Proper nouns always begin with a capital letter. Find the proper nouns below.

Many people lived east of the **Mississippi River** in 1800.

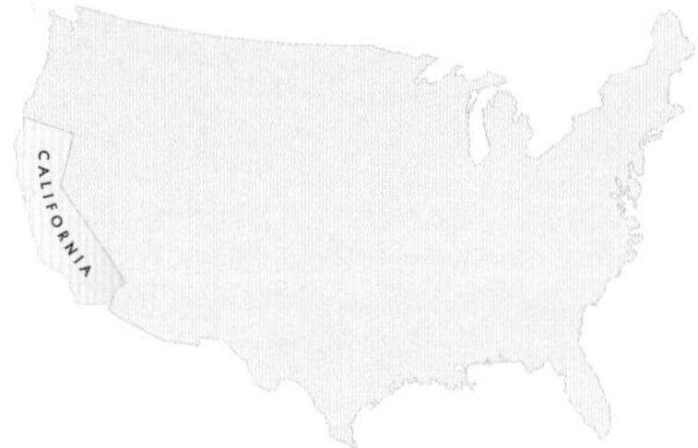

People discovered gold in **California.**

Many settlers traveled west on the **Oregon Trail.**

Thomas Jefferson bought land that doubled the size of the country.

Multiple-Meaning Words

Some words have more than one meaning. Think about the two meanings for each of these words. Then use each word in a sentence of your own.

The discovery of gold **drew** people west.

The boy **drew** a picture.

It is not easy to **cross** a river in a covered wagon.

My mother looked **cross** when I misbehaved.

Traveling in a covered wagon is **hard** work.

The rocks on the mountain are **hard.**

Research and Write

Write About the West

Lewis and Clark made the first trip across what is today the United States. Find out more about their trip. How many people went? How did they travel? How long was the trip?

Research

Collect books and reference materials, or go online.

Read and Take Notes

As you read, take notes and draw pictures.

Write

Then write an informational report about the expedition of Lewis and Clark.

Read and Compare

Read More About the West

Find and read other books about the western United States. As you read, think about these questions.

- How is the West different from where you live?
- How is the West similar to where you live?
- Are there places in the West you want to visit?

Books to Read

▲ Read the letters of one family as they traveled along the Oregon Trail.

▲ Discover the history and culture of the western United States.

▲ Learn more about the building of the transcontinental railroad.

Glossary

churn (page 20)
To mix or stir milk to make butter
Bumping along the trail churned the milk.

draw (page 12)
To attract
In 1848, the discovery of gold draws people west.

KEY CONCEPT

expedition (page 9)
A journey or trip to explore a new place
Lewis and Clark led the expedition.

KEY CONCEPT

frontier (page 7)
Unexplored land at the edge of a settled area
The land in the West was a frontier.

KEY CONCEPT

hardship (page 15)
A problem
Settlers faced many hardships on the trail.

KEY CONCEPT

Homestead Act (page 13)
A law that gave land to settlers
The United States government passed the Homestead Act in 1862.

KEY CONCEPT

settler (page 11)
A person who moves to an undeveloped area to live
Many early settlers moved west for farmland.

tribe (page 10)
A group of people or families living together
Many Native American tribes lived in the West.

Index